The World Turned Rightside Up:
A New Trading Agenda for the Age of Globalisation

John C. Hulsman

With commentaries by

Professor Patrick Minford

Martin Howe QC

The Rt. Hon. David Davis MP

Bill Jamieson

Occasional Paper 114

Published by the Institute of Economic Affairs, 2001

First published in January 2001 by
The Institute of Economic Affairs
2 Lord North Street
Westminster
London SW1P 3LB

© The Institute of Economic Affairs 2001

Occasional Paper 114
ISBN 0-255 36495-4

Many IEA publications are translated into languages other
than English or are reprinted. Permission to translate or to
reprint should be sought from the General Director at the
address above.

Printed in Great Britain by Hartington Fine Arts Limited,
Lancing, West Sussex

Set in Times Roman 12 on 14 point

Contents

Acknowledgements

John Hulsman gratefully acknowledges the significant contribution made to the development of this paper by: Gerald P. O'Driscoll Jr., Director of The Heritage Foundation's Center For International Trade and Economics (CITE); Aaron Schavey, Economic Policy Analyst, CITE; Denise Froning, Economic Policy Analyst, CITE; Michael Scardaville, Research Assistant, The Heritage Foundation's Kathryn and Shelby Cullom Davis Institute for International Studies; and Brett Schaefer, Jay Kingham Fellow in International Regulatory Affairs, CITE.

Foreword

In the Spring of 2000, the Institute arranged a visit by two senior members of The Heritage Foundation in Washington—Dr Gerald P. O'Driscoll Jr., Director of the Foundation's Center for International Trade and Economics and Dr John C.Hulsman, Senior Policy Analyst in European Affairs in the Kathryn and Shelby Cullom Davis Institute for International Studies. Dr Hulsman gave several lectures in London, based on a paper he had written which suggested that Britain join the United States in forming a global Free Trade Association which any country committed to a liberal trade order could join. Dr Hulsman put forward his proposal as an alternative for Britain to ever-closer integration with the rest of the EU.

At a time when public opposition to Britain's joining the euro was increasing, and a debate was emerging about the long term costs and benefits of Britain's membership of the EU, Dr Hulsman's proposal aroused considerable interest. Some commentators welcomed it as a positive proposal which, if implemented, would permit Britain to gain the benefits of freer trade whilst avoiding a constant battle with EU partners which had the ultimate aim of political integration and therefore kept making proposals consistent with that aim. Others, however, cautioned against the problems which would arise if Britain, as a member of a customs union, attempted to join a free trade area: the consequences, it was said, would be a messy and acrimonious withdrawal by Britain from the EU which would be disruptive for both sides.

To move the debate forward, and in particular to test whether or not Dr Hulsman's proposal represents the positive alternative to the EU sought by a growing number of British people, we asked four well-known writers on European Union issues to analyse the idea and write commentaries on it. The result is Occasional Paper 114 which begins with Dr Hulsman's paper, is followed by commentaries by Professor Patrick Minford, Martin Howe QC, the Rt Hon David Davis MP and Bill Jamieson, and concludes with a response by Dr Hulsman. All the commentators are generally supportive of the Hulsman idea, though they differ on the form any wider free trade area might take and on the appropriate timing of any such move. One of the papers, by Martin Howe QC, provides a remarkably clear account of how to deal with one of the principal issues the Hulsman paper raises—how to overcome the obstacles to participating in wider free trade which are inherent in Britain's membership of the EU.

The views expressed are those of the authors, not of the Institute (which has no corporate view), its Managing Trustees, Academic Advisory Council members or senior staff. But most readers will conclude that this Occasional Paper stands out in the discussions about Britain's relationship with the European Union, not only by raising issues of real substance rather than ephemera, but by providing positive suggestions about a way out of the confused and quarrelsome state into which that relationship appears to have relapsed.

December 2000   COLIN ROBINSON
Editorial Director, Institute of Economic Affairs
Professor of Economics, University of Surrey

The Authors

Dr. John C. Hulsman, is the Senior Policy Analyst in European Affairs in the Kathryn and Shelby Cullom Davis Institute for International Studies at The Heritage Foundation, Washington DC. Dr. Hulsman focuses on European security and NATO affairs, the European Union, European politics and economics and US-European trade and economic relations.

Dr. Hulsman started his career teaching World Politics and US Foreign Policy at the University of St. Andrews, Scotland. In this and subsequent capacities Dr. Hulsman has been published and interviewed many times regarding issues vital to trans-Atlantic relations in the post-Cold War era. Prior to joining Heritage, Dr. Hulsman was a fellow in European studies at the Center for Strategic and International Studies in Washington DC, where he specialised in US-European political, economic and military links in the post-Cold War era.

Dr Hulsman is the author, *inter alia*, of *A Paradigm for the New World Order; A Schools of Thought Analysis of American Foreign Policy in the Post-Cold War Era* (Macmillan 1997) and *A Grand Bargain with Europe, Preserving NATO for the 21st Century*, (The Heritage Foundation 2000).

Patrick Minford, is Professor of Applied Economics, Cardiff Business School, University of Wales at Cardiff. From 1976-1997, he was Professor of Applied Economics at Liverpool University. He was a member of the Monopolies and Mergers Commission 1990-96 and one of H M Treasury's Panel of Forecasters ('Six Wise Men') January

1993-December 1996. He was awarded the CBE for services to economics, 1996. He is the author of books and articles on exchange rates, unemployment, housing and macro-economics and has an occasional column in *The Daily Telegraph*.

Martin Howe is a practising Queen's Counsel specialising in European law and intellectual property law, who conducts cases in the English courts, the European Court of Justice and other European tribunals. He has written extensively on the effects of the European Treaties and on related legal and constitutional matters.

Previous publications include *Europe and the Constitution after Maastricht* (Nelson & Pollard, Oxford, 1993); *Monetary Policy after Maastricht* (Centre for Policy Studies, 1992); *Maastricht and 'Social Europe': an Escape or an Entrapment?* (1993); and *Better Off Out? The Benefits or Costs of EU Membership* (IEA, 1996, jointly with Brian Hindley).

The Rt Hon David Davis is Member of Parliament for Haltemprice and Howden. He has been a Member of Parliament since 1987. He was Minister for Europe from 1994 to 1997, and is currently Chairman of the House of Commons Public Accounts Committee.

Bill Jamieson, formerly Economics Editor of *The Sunday Telegraph*, is now Executive Editor of *The Scotsman* and Director of the Edinburgh-based Policy Institute. He has written extensively on Europe and co-authored with Professor Patrick Minford *Britain and Europe: Choices for Change*, published in 1999 by Politeia.

The World Turned Rightside Up: A New Trading Agenda for the Age of Globalization

John C. Hulsman

Not very far from Washington, almost 220 years ago, General Lord Charles Cornwallis found himself in a bit of bother due to the ragtag Continental army under General George Washington. After the heroic night storming of one of his outer redoubts by Colonel Alexander Hamilton, Cornwallis realized that he was obliged to surrender his army of British grenadiers, the finest infantrymen in the world, to the upstart colonists. This was a fact the noble-born Cornwallis simply could not face. Rather than enduring the social humiliation of surrendering in person to Washington, Cornwallis feigned illness to avoid the surrender ceremony altogether. Washington, the scion of one of Virginia's oldest families, was quick to recognize the slight; he sent his second-in-command, General Lincoln, to meet with Cornwallis' stand-in, General O'Hara. As the British troops marched by their American conquerors, the British military band, reflecting what must have been the utter disbelief of the British army, played the tune, The World Turned Upside Down.

Since that fateful encounter on the banks of the James (with the notable exception of The War of 1812), Anglo-American ties have recovered, especially during the Twentieth Century. It is no exaggeration to say that America has no more proven or dependable an ally than Great Britain. History has underscored the commonalities of the relationship with ties built on common language, common history, and common culture. It is hard to imagine another two powers having shared interests as compatible as the descendents of Lord Cornwallis and his worthy adversary.

Yet now this seemingly unshakable relationship is being called into question. A seminal decision regarding its future awaits Britain early in the new century. A referendum on Britain's entry into the euro-zone may occur as early as the next parliament. A yes vote would irrevocably merge British sovereignty into a larger European supranational construct, if the rhetoric of the current Euro-zone members is to be believed. This is, quite simply, the last real chance for Britain to choose an alternate future path, one that recognises that its natural economic and political partner remains the United States and not the European Union.

British Hesitations About The European Experiment

Such a shift has its origin firmly planted in modern-day realities. When asked in a November 1999 *Economist* poll who was the UK's most reliable ally in a crisis, 59% of those polled said the US, with only 16% paying Europe that compliment. There is no doubt that the people of the UK remain deeply sceptical about the euro in particular and the European experiment in general. For instance, the unpopular Tories, albeit on a low turnout, stunningly won the Euro-elections of summer 1999 by making them a referendum on joining the euro. A January 2000 ICM survey in *The Guardian* showed a record 63% of the voters opposed to euro membership and only 25% in favour. Nor is even remaining in the European Union beyond question. An ICM survey for *Business for Sterling* of 1,000 adults taken just before Christmas 1999 shows that 46% of voters favour leaving the EU altogther, an 8 percent increase on a similar poll taken 6 months earlier. People in the UK remain profoundly sceptical of Europe and the euro; this dissatisfaction will lead them, sooner or later, to cast about for a viable alternative to being swallowed by the EU. Thus, the notion of closer Anglo-American trade ties is destined to play well in the UK.

Despite these figures, the Labour Party platform has

committed the government to call for a referendum on the euro, probably in the life of the next parliament. Assuming the Conservatives campaign for a no vote in a euro referendum, however well they put their argument, however skilfuly they deconstruct the yes case, their task is an essentially destructive rather than a creative one. This is a charge that has dogged conservatism in both the US and UK since the glory days of Reagan and Thatcher; one knows what conservatives are against, but what are they for? This damning question is invariably what Labour is bound to ask in the upcoming British referendum. Silence is not an effective answer, either politically or intellectually.

My proposal is that, as an alternative to Prime Minister Blair's 'third way' push for ever closer integration with Europe, we should rally round a rival standard: Britain's entry into a global Free Trade Association (FTA), with the US and the UK as charter members. Such a plan requires the UK to shift its politico-economic focus from Europe and instead return its gaze to what is clearly the most successful partnership of the twentieth century—the special relationship between the UK of Cornwallis and the US of Hamilton and Washington. A Free Trade Association represents the kind of international institution conservatives ought to favour; a coalition of the willing determined to maximise trade liberalisation throughout our member states.

The American Case for Closer US-UK Trade Links

Beyond providing the British with a compelling political alternative to euro membership, there are several general reasons such an Association makes sense from an American point of view. First, the US is already deeply commercially enmeshed with Britain; further trade liberalisation would result in immediate and significant benefits for the American economy. In 1997 British direct investment in the US was $18.3 billion, greater than any other country's, and 30% of the total of all foreign direct investment in the US. America invested more in Britain than anywhere else—$22.4 billion, or 20% of the total of all US FDI. This pattern continued into 1999, wherein British institutions invested £107 billion in companies overseas. Of that, 31% was in the other 14 nations of the EU and a full 60% was in the US alone.[1] Also, sterling has tended to move far more in line with the dollar than with the euro. This greatly affects interest rate harmonisation, with American and British rates being 6% and the European Central Bank setting rates at 3.5% early in 2000. This leads to the inescapable conclusion that the American and British economies are more in-sync with one another than either is with the economic powers on the Continent.

The changed nature of the post-Cold War era itself has made a significant US-UK economic link possible. Being close, as the UK is to the continent, no longer translates into greater volume of financial interactions compared with trade with a country far away, as it has done throughout history. In the new era, the concept of location has been transformed as the result of the telecommunications revolution that is such a salient characteristic of the age of globalisation. To some extent the Internet has epitomised this death of distance. The centrality of an US-UK trade link would not have worked nearly so well in the age of the sailing ship, or even when the Treaty of Rome was signed in 1957. But globalisation has made such a link very possible as the above economic figures indicate.

Second, the US and the UK share a common politico-economic culture; this makes a trade combination between them far more likely to prove economically successful. In the era of globalisation, the world can best be assessed as divided into three camps, exhibiting markedly different strains of capitalism: Statists, Reaganite/Thatcherites, with advocates of the third way vainly trying to square the circle of finding a coherent middle way between the two. Germany and France,

---

[1]   Michael Fabricant, 'US a Tempting Alternative to EU', *The Times*, 15 February 2000.

with their reliance on a massive role for the state in their economies, lavish tax and benefits systems, structurally high unemployment (the US unemployment rate is less than half that of France, Italy, Spain, and Germany) and greater tendency toward protectionism, are clearly statist in politico-economic culture. A most curious phenomenon is that the statist model has been dominant on the continent; all the major parties in both France and Germany share a common antipathy to the Reagan/Thatcherite model. This is not the case in the UK; Prime Minister Tony Blair has done little to overturn the effects of the Thatcher revolution relating to privatisation, deregulation, and a more market-oriented approach. It is simply a fact of life that continental Europe is largely statist and that this politico-economic orientation is increasingly incompatible with the Anglo-Saxon form of capitalism.

No two countries in the world are closer economically and politically than the United States and the United Kingdom. It is not simply that the British were the dominant original settlers of US, though that matters. What matters more, however, is the political traditions and institutions that the early British colonists brought with them: the Magna Carta, the Common Law legal system, and the political rights embedded in that system. Out of this background came the idea for a written constitution to protect these inalienable rights. But the rights themselves and their intellectual justification came directly from British political thought.

The Anglo-American culture of freedom is one that values the individual in politics and economics.[2] Politically, that tradition translates into an anti-statist ethos favouring limited government; that ethos supports the rights of citizens and their representatives over that of centralised power. In the United States, it led to the displacement of the monarchy

---

2 Friedrich A; Hayek, 'Individualism: True and False', in Friedrich A. Hayek, *Individualism and Economic Order*, Chicago: University of Chicago Press, 1948.

itself; in the United Kingdom, the monarchy was merely circumscribed constitutionally.

Economically, individualism leads to entrepreneurship and innovation, invention and prosperity, growth and development. It is no accident that the freest economies in the world have generally adopted the Anglo-American capitalist model of development with its openness to foreign trade and investment. According to The Heritage Foundation's *2000 Index of Economic Freedom* the 10 freest economies in the world are in order: Hong Kong; Singapore; New Zealand; Bahrain; Luxembourg; the US; Ireland; Australia; Switzerland; and the UK.[3] Of these, 7 of the freest countries are former colonies of an 8th, the United Kingdom (Bahrain, the United States, Australia, New Zealand, Hong Kong, Singapore and Ireland). Switzerland also ranks highly partly due to an Anglo-American link; the Swiss adopted their own variant of federalism and individual freedom when they modeled their Constitution after that of the United States.

The culture of freedom can flourish whenever a great society of free people merges, engendering a self-confidence that permits a nation to open itself not only to an inflow of goods, but also ideas and practices. In no other two countries has that culture flourished for so long and so successfully as it has in the United States and the United Kingdom. Nowhere can the disparity between economic freedom and statism be more obviously seen than in comparing the economic systems on each side of the English Channel. Any historical look at the UK's long-evidenced frustrations with the EU bears out the difficulties of unlike forms of capitalism banding together. The US and the UK exhibit an anti-statist, pro-free trade, pro-markets politico-economic culture; sharing a common school of thought makes a trade combination infinitely more likely to be successful and is a strong argument in favour of a new trade combination between the US and the UK.

---

[3] 'Business This Week', *The Economist*, 4 December 1999.

From an American point of view, an expanding, global free trade association clustered around the US and the UK would have a great competitive economic advantage over the EU due to this shared politico-economic culture. The Anglo-American anti-statist politico-economic cultural model is the principal reason that between 1993-7 net employment in the US rose by 8%, while in the Europe it remained flat.[4] Over nineteen million jobs were created in the US in the 1990s. Dismally, the countries adopting the euro ran a net loss of private sector jobs in the 1990s. This is due to the EU's more corporatist approach, as statism advocates a larger role for the government in the marketplace, a padded safety net and, correspondingly, espouses a greater advocacy of protectionist doctrines to shield these inefficient practices. This has led to a European-wide economic crisis in the past decade, as Europe has found it more and more difficult to compete worldwide. Using the Heritage Index, the US is currently the 6th freest economy in the world, while the weighted euroland average places it 28th. This is a direct result of the EU's adherence to the less competitive statist politico-economic cultural model.[5] As Yergin and Stanislaw argue, in Europe, 'The overextended welfare system undermines the ability to create the wealth required to pay for it.'[6] This remains statism's greatest conceptual flaw, and stands in stark contrast to the increased economic dynamism that closer trade links with the UK would provide America.

Excessive regulation is the second mortal blow to statism; as US Treasury Secretary, Larry Summers, notes, 'it takes 12 times longer to set up a new business in Europe than in the US, and 4 times the cost.'[7] The price of such excessive

---

4   Daniel Yergin and Joseph Stanislaw, *The Commanding Heights*, New York: Simon and Schuster, 1998, p. 321.

5   J.T. Young, 'Euro's Economics Lesson', *The Washington Times*, 18 January 2000.

6   Yergin and Stanislaw, *The Commanding Heights*, op. cit., p. 323.

7   Martin Wolf, 'Europe's Growth Opportunity', *The Financial Times*, 10 September 1999.

regulation is the stifling of economic growth. The Anglo-American economic culture exhibits a greater advocacy of free trade, a more dynamic economic environment, and a limited safety net. Such a grouping will inevitably fare better in the new era, driven as it is by markets and economic fundamentals. Such has proven to be the case. Taking the euro-zone as a whole, there have been only three quarters since the second half of 1992 when year-on-year growth has been stronger in Europe than in the US.[8] Also, unemployment in the euro-zone is double that of America, and the euro has experienced massive capital flight since its inception, dramatically driving its value downwards. In terms of politico-economic culture in the age of globalization (to say nothing of the advantage a common language bestows), a free trade area centred on an Anglo-American nexus is simply a better fit for both countries than any conceivable alternate economic arrangements.

Nor should the European Union as an institution be looked to as the vanguard of economic reform, and a reason why Britain should shun a closer trading link with the US. While there are undoubtedly some aspects of Brussels that favour a more open economy, the majority of the characteristics of the EU pull in the opposite, statist direction. The EU's Common Agricultural Policy (CAP), which consumes around half of the entire EU budget, accounts for 85% of total global agricultural subsidies.[9] Patrick Messerlin, a leading French economist, calculated that trade protectionism costs the EU between 6 and 7% of its GDP per annum, some $600 billion, or equal to the annual economic output of Spain.[10] This protectionism ranges far beyond merely agriculture, proving

---

[8] Tony Barber, 'A Political Will for Reform', *The Financial Times*, 10 September 1999.

[9] Adam Entous, 'Labour Groups Challenge WTO on Trade Round', *Reuters*, 29 November 1999.

[10] Guy de Jonquieres, 'Protectionism is Costing EU 6% of GDP', *The Financial Times*, 10 November 1999.

just as prevalent in the manufacturing, textiles, and clothing sectors. Structural and regional funds for the less developed members of the union have proven to be national feeding troughs, thinly disguised forms of excessive subsidisation of national economies. The Social Chapter, and generally attempts at harmonisation, have been used as tools to protect over-generous French and German labour legislation against the competitive pressures from smaller, poorer European countries that may have initially had an economic advantage in that they had less regulated labour markets. An organisation marked by these characteristics cannot be thought of as a tool designed to liberalise a sclerotic Europe, and thus is not in American interests.

Third, from an American point of view the Anglo-American grouping will also politically protect the US from whatever the outcome of the European experiment in supranationalism. I wish to make it clear that I am not against 'Europe'; I am against a protectionist Euro-Federal grouping. We need to be as clear-eyed about this as the French and Germans are. They have no trouble reconciling the ambiguity that the US is both an ally and a rival of theirs; such are the complexities of the world. Robert Cottrell accurately sums up the current French stereotype of America,

'Once the main threat came from the USSR. Now it comes from globalization, portrayed in France as an American-led process of leveling down in which quantity is allowed to destroy quality and market forces to undermine good government. The correct defense is a Europe rich in protectionism and global control.'[11]

Nor is this a minority view, as is sometimes claimed. A poll conducted in France by CSA in April 1999 showed that 68% of the French said they were worried about Americas status as a superpower. Only 30% said there was anything to admire

---

[11] Robert Cottrell, 'Once and Future Leaders', *The Economist*, 23 October 1999.

across the Atlantic.[12] Nor is there a genuine teleological argument here; there is no doubt that a major strain of Euro-federalism is anti-American in its thrust. We need to stop thinking that French rhetoric is not serious, that it is just a cultural eccentricity. Rather, it reflects the honest beliefs of a people who have a very different political and economic agenda from that of the United States.

This makes the tired and complacent words of support for the EU emanating from the Clinton administration all the more galling. There is a danger for the US if the EU proves to be too successful in its attempts at centralisation. If it succeeds in becoming some sort of coherent federal structure, it may well try to sever the transatlantic link, as Henry Kissinger has suggested[13], even attempting to become a rival hegemon in the long-term. This is fundamentally not in America's interests. There is little doubt that such a goal is the object of many European centralisers. Georges-Marc Benamou, in *Le Dernier Mitterand*, has the elderly French President saying,

'France does not know it, but we are at war with America. Yes, a permanent war, a vital war, a war without death. Yes, they are very hard the Americans, they are voracious, they want undivided power over the world.'[14]

Likewise Gerhard Schroeder, in a television interview December 28, 1999, said, 'Whining about US dominance does not help, we have to act.' He then went on to advocate that Europe must act more like a single country if it wants to challenge US economic and political dominance.[15] As Dr.

---

[12] Suzanne Daley, 'Europe's Dim View of US is Evolving into Frank Hostility', *The New York Times*, 9 April 2000.

[13] Conrad Black, 'Britain's Atlantic Option – And America's Stake', *National Interest*, No. 55, Spring 1999, pp. 21-22.

[14] Conrad Black, *ibid.*, p. 22.

[15] 'Schroeder to Europe: Unite vs. US', *Associated Press*, 28 December 1999.

Kissinger noted, as the preponderant power in the world, it is precisely such a challenge, from however seemingly benign a source, that America must be prepared to counter.[16]

Stormy Times Ahead for the US-EU Relationship?

For it is almost beyond question that stormy times lie ahead for the US-EU relationship. This is largely because they espouse differing and often competing forms of capitalism. As Hindley notes, trade policy is a reflection of the polity deploying it.[17] I quite agree with Pascal Lamy, the EU's Trade Representative, that trade disputes, such as the current row over genetically modified foods, stem from deep moral and cultural differences between the US and the EU.[18] These significant differences are both reflected and exacerbated by the different economic schools of thought espoused by Brussels and Washington. For the very institutional structure of the EU illustrates that the more integrated Europe is, the more protectionist its leanings become. The external activity in which the Union is most perfectly integrated is regarding trade policy, where, for all practical purposes, Europe behaves as if it were a sovereign state. It is also the area in which the EU and America disagree most fiercely. From an American point of view, this is not an encouraging advertisement for further European integration.[19]

The reasons for the EU espousing a generally more protectionist trading line should be obvious; its economic model is not as competitive as the American strain of capitalism. This does not mean that the EU does not have policy choices. As *The Economist* states, 'Even if American

[16] Henry Kissinger, *Diplomacy*, New York: Simon and Schuster, 1994, p. 813.

[17] Brian Hindley, 'Liberalism and Illiberalism in the New Era', in Jeffrey Gedmin (ed.), *European Integration and American Interests*, Washington, DC: The AEI Press, 1997, p. 21.

[18] Guy de Jonquieres, 'Liberal with a Social Mission [Interview with Pascal Lamy]', *The Financial Times*, 21 October 1999.

[19] Robert Cottrell, 'Here's the Beef', *The Economist*, 23 October 1999.

capitalism is the best way to get rich, nothing in the logic of globalisation forces other countries to adopt the American way if they would rather be different and accept the cost.'[20] This should perhaps read reapportion the cost, in this case primarily to consumers within Europe itself by artificially protecting European markets from genuinely open competition with America. Given the inefficiencies inherent in the EUs statist politico-economic model, Europe will find it increasingly hard to compete in the era of globalisation. Protectionism is the most obvious answer to the EUs economic dilemma; such a policy is obviously not in American interests.

In many ways then, the current increasingly rocky relationship between the US and the EU signals the final failure of America's 40-year-old policy toward Brussels. The Clinton Administration has continued to endorse the long-held false vision that a Britain at the centre of increased European integration (symbolised at the moment by adoption of the euro) will somehow tame the Franco-German axis by transforming it over time into a more pro-free market, pro-trade, pro-American entity. Instead, if anything, the reverse has held true. Brussels has obliged Britain to support policies that are less pro-free trade, less pro-free market, less pro-American. The Blair government's adoption of the Social Chapter is the latest illustration that, if anything, the Franco-German axis is poised to make inroads into Britain's different politico-economic culture, rather than vice-versa. Britain will not play a decisive role in what becomes of the EU (as always, that will be left to Germany and France) but it can play a critical role in assuring that an American-led bloc will maintain its dominance by a wide margin over such an integrated statist rival.

---

[20] *The Economist*, 'One True Model?', 8 April 2000.

The Way Ahead

The political way ahead for this revolutionary new trade nexus is straightforward. After campaigning for the euro option in the context of an EMU referendum in the life of the next parliament and losing, the Blair government will either fall or be gravely weakened, as it is so closely associated with entry into the Euro-zone. Either with a desperately weakened Blair or a Tory government, flush with triumph after winning the referendum, Britain's entry into a Free Trade Association with the US becomes the logical policy alternative. Britain, in line with the current Conservative position, should attempt to renegotiate the Treaty of Rome, allowing it opt-outs over all pieces of legislation relating to further losses of sovereignty and the ability to enter into bilateral trade negotiations with the US to join such a FTA. I believe such talks are certainly desirable from a British point of view. I want to make this very clear; there is no objective reason the UK's entry into an FTA should be an either/or proposition regarding its continued membership within the EU. If the union really is the benign organisation it claims to be, it should welcome the further global trade liberalisation and pro-American stance such a new organisation would profess. It is only if Brussels has a hidden anti-American, protectionist agenda that it ought to object to such an initiative. Given what the EU has been telling us all along, surely this cannot be possible?

In reality, of course, such an outcome is more than possible. As Geoffrey Martin, the European Commission's representative in London stated, reacting to the present more pro-sovereignty Tory policy 'The Conservative Approach was detached from the real circumstances of the EU.'[21] He pointed out that the trend in the EU was to extend its remit; I take him at his word. If the EU really wants to go forward with an ever-closer union, currently symbolised by adoption

---

[21] Robert Peston, 'Opposition Party Commits to Altering EU Treaty', *The Financial Times*, 6 October 1999.

of the euro, it will press on whatever Britain decides to do. Only in such a situation should the UK contemplate leaving the union.

If negotiations fail, even then Britain should attempt to retain the obvious benefits of belonging to the single market. It should then re-enter EFTA, joining the European Economic Area (EEA) along with Norway, Iceland, and Liechtenstein, which is the linking of the single markets of the EU and willing EFTA members, excepting matters relating to the Common Agricultural Policy and fisheries.[22] Such a link would preserve British sovereignty (a vital political concern), keep the UK in the single market, while allowing it to negotiate a closer trading status with the US. EEA membership entails no transfer of legislative power from the parliaments of contracting parties to EEA institutions. Decisions by the EEA joint committee (composed of EU and EEA members) in principle need to be transposed into national legislation to be binding in each EFTA country. Again, only if the other member states of the EU refuse to allow Britain to make its own sovereign decision regarding initiating closer US-UK trade links, does a fundamental choice need to be made.

A Shared Commitment to Increasing Trade

A global Free Trade Association (FTA) will be founded on a genuine shared commitment to increasing trade between its member states and at a global level. It will serve as a practical advertisement for the enduring global benefits of free trade as the benefits of such an association become apparent; an example all the more precious in the wake of the Seattle WTO debacle. It could come to encompass such countries as New Zealand, Hong Kong, Bahrain, Ireland, Chile, Singapore, Israel, Denmark, Luxembourg, Estonia and the Czech Republic. The Free Trade Association will be a voluntary and

---

[22] Conrad Black, 'Britain's Atlantic Option', *op. cit.*, p. 18.

inclusive grouping, whose expanded membership should be based solely on a policy commitment by its member states to a genuinely liberal global trading order. The plan embraces a commitment to a state's sovereignty. Its economic policies (and the choices they represent) will determine whether or not it qualifies for the grouping.

This commitment will be characterized by a state's meeting certain numerical targets (such as those used in the methodology employed in The Heritage Foundation's *Index of Economic Freedom–2000*) regarding a country's openness, relating to its trade policy, capital flows and investment, property rights and low level of regulation (for details of the plan, see Appendix pp. 25-28). Members will thus select themselves based on their genuine commitment to a liberal trading order. It is hoped that membership will quickly grow, as a further 23 countries are within sight of the numerical target for accession (including Australia, Canada, Jamaica, Uruguay, Poland, Latvia, Turkey, and Lithuania). Given my firm belief in the economic superiority of the Anglo-American economic model, such an organisation will have a disproportionate number of English-speaking members, certainly in the short- and medium-term. However, the numerical target concept allows for self-selection, giving the whole project an inclusivity it would otherwise lack, while advancing our common desire to strengthen the ties that bind the English-speaking world together. The Free Trade Association's internal initiatives will include: freer movement of capital within the new grouping; establishing common accounting standards; setting uniform numerically-driven very low rates of subsidy, as well as diminishing overt and hidden tariffs.

This new Anglo-American economic tie will simply build upon the older links that have made this relationship one of the most fruitful and enduring in history. This plan exemplifies conservatism at its Burkean best, proposing policies based on conditions that already exist rather than, as with the EU, trying to legislate sand castles in the sky into reality. For an indication of the vibrancy of the Anglo-American tie lies in its duration. As Churchill observed during The Battle of Britain, August 20, 1940:

'The British Empire and the United States will have to be somewhat mixed up together in some of their affairs for mutual and general advantage. For my own part, looking out across the future, I do not view the process with any misgivings. I could not stop it if I wished; no one can stop it. Like the Mississippi it just keeps rolling along. Let it roll. Let it roll on full flood, inexorable, irresistible, benignant, to broader lands and better days.'

Let us heed this hallowed voice, preserving and enhancing this vital link, which has seen us through so much in the past and can be a source of so much in the future.

Appendix

Proposed Criteria for becoming a member of
The Free Trade Association
Compiled with Aaron Schavey, Economic Policy
Analyst, The Heritage Foundation

Membership in the Free Trade Association (FTA) is entirely voluntary and is not an abridgement of sovereignty in any way; members can choose to withdraw from the trading regime freely. The only other way to be removed from the regime is to cease to meet the numerical standards that, unlike those relating to euro membership, cannot be finessed. The FTA will be founded around a genuine commitment to increasing free trade between its member states and at the global level. This commitment will be characterised by a state's meeting certain numerical targets regarding a country's openness relating to its trade policy, capital flows and investment, property rights, and low level of regulation. These categories fall into four broad areas that characterise a country's commitment to a genuinely liberal trading order: a) freedom to trade, b) freedom to invest, c) freedom to operate a business without excessive burdens, d) and security in the investment.

To ensure that FTA members are genuinely committed to free trade and that expanding trade with the countries in the trading regime can realistically be achieved, the following criteria based on the *2000 Index of Economic Freedom* are proposed.[a]

Countries seeking FTA membership status should:

Freedom to Trade

Receive a score of either 1 or 2 on trade policy.[b] Countries with a score of 1 or 2 maintain average tariff rates below 9% and have low non-tariff barriers. For example, countries with low non-tariff barriers generally do not use import quotas or licensing requirements to restrict trade.

Freedom to Invest

Receive a score of either 1 or 2 on capital flows and investment[c], which is equivalent to countries possessing an accessible foreign investment code, treating foreign investment openly and impartially, and maintaining an efficient approval process. The only investment restrictions permitted for FTA membership status are some restrictions on investments in utilities, companies vital to national security and natural resources.

---

[a] The choice to use the Heritage Index over other measures of a country's commitment to a liberal trading order does not bias the selection of the FTA membership. *The Index of Economic Freedom* is highly correlated with the Fraser Institute's *Economic Freedom of the World* and Freedom House's *World Survey of Economic Freedom*. Steve Hanke and Stephen Walters estimate the Spearman rank correlation coefficient for the Heritage Foundation Index with the Fraser Institute survey and the Freedom House survey and find that they equal 0.85 and 0.82 respectively. See Stephen H. Hanke and Stephen J.K. Walters, 'Economic Freedom, Prosperity, and Equality: A Survey', *Cato Journal*, Vol. 17, No. 2, Fall 1997, p. 135.

[b] Countries that score a 1 on trade policy have an average tariff rate of less than or equal to 4 per cent and/or very low non-tariff barriers. Countries that score a 2 have an average tariff rate of greater than 4 per cent but less than or equal to 9 per cent and/or low non-tariff barriers.

[c] Countries that score a 1 on capital flows and investment treat foreign investment openly and impartially and have an accessible foreign investment code. Countries that score a 2 impose restrictions on investments like utilities, companies vital to national security, and natural resources; they also maintain a limited, efficient approval process.

26

Freedom to Operate a Business

Receive a score of either 1 or 2 on regulation.[d] A country that has excessively burdensome regulations could deter trade. Investors may choose not to invest in a country because of the problems of opening a business or the high cost of doing business in a country. Countries that score either a 1 or a 2 on regulation maintain simple licensing procedures and apply regulations uniformly.

Secure Property Rights

Receive a score of either 1 or 2 on property rights.[e] A country with well-established rule of law protects private property and provides an environment where business transactions can take place with a degree of certainty. Investors are more likely to engage in economic transactions when they know the judicial system protects private property and is not subject to outside influence.

Countries that generally set low tariff barriers and do not use excessive non-tariff barriers and do not put serious impediments in the way of foreign investment exhibit a fundamental commitment to free trade. It is important for countries to secure property rights and desist from excessively burdensome regulations as this ensures that expanding trade with such a country within the FTA trading regime can be realistically achieved. Countries that maintain an adequate

---

[d] Countries that receive a 1 on regulation have regulations that are straightforward and applied uniformly to all businesses; regulations are not much of a burden for business; corruption is nearly non-existent. Countries that receive a 2 maintain simple licensing procedures; existing regulations are relatively straightforward and are applied uniformly most of the time, but are still burdensome in some instances; corruption, although possible, is rare and not a significant national problem.

[e] Countries that score a 1 on property rights have a government that guarantees private property, administers an efficient court system that enforces contracts and a justice system that punishes those who unlawfully confiscate private property. Expropriation of private property is unlikely. Countries that receive a 2 have a government that guarantees private property, but enforcement is lax in some cases. Expropriation of private property is unlikely.

rule of law that protects private property encourage trade and investment. Investors are more likely to put their money in a country where the judicial system is transparent and enforces contracts. In addition, businesses are more likely to invest their money where regulations are not burdensome and where they are applied uniformly.

Based on the above-mentioned criteria, 12 countries in addition to the United States presently qualify for FTA member status: Bahrain, Chile, the Czech Republic, Denmark, Estonia, Hong Kong, Ireland, Israel, Luxembourg, New Zealand, Singapore, United Kingdom.

Twenty-three further countries are within one point (using the Heritage scoring system) of reaching the FTA standards. If they choose to do so and follow slightly more liberal trade policies, such countries ought to be able to join the FTA in the near future. They are: Australia, Canada, Jamaica, Uruguay, Peru, Bolivia, Switzerland, Austria, the Netherlands, Belgium, Iceland, Finland, Germany, Italy, Norway, Portugal, Sweden, Spain, Latvia, Greece, Turkey, Poland and Lithuania.

Commentary:
A Loose, Co-operative Alliance of Like-Minded Nations
Patrick Minford

I warmly applaud this paper. Let me underline one sentence (out of hundreds of excellent ones):

> 'If the union really is the benign organisation it claims to be, it should welcome the further global trade liberalisation and pro-American stance such a new organisation would profess.' (p. 21)

Yes, indeed; amen and again amen.

The problem is this: for years the UK has gone along with the EU in a rationalist spirit of 'come on, let's build the free market you all agree we want.' As is well known, the Single Market was Margaret Thatcher's legacy to the EU, pushed forward by Lord Cockfield with her fullest support. Jacques Delors also backed it, presumably as a means to increase the centralising powers of the EU; and no sooner was the ink dry than he brought in the raft of Social Charter proposals whose thrust was diametrically opposed to the liberalising intentions of the Single Market. Like a spreading poison, these proposals now inform and pollute most of the EU's activities; the latest terrifying idea embodied in the Social Chapter is that of pan-European union rights and bargaining. In an era of 'globalization' in which capitalism has supposedly 'ended history' we find ourselves in the EU dragged into the heart of an ideological throwback process. Accompanying this 'social

democrat'/ 'socialist'/ 'third way' (words to taste) pro-
gramme is a not-so-covert anti-Americanism and desire for a
rival European imperium.

My words will be dismissed by the broad alliance on the
'moderate left' in this country pushing for our greater
integration into this project; they will say I am the ideological
one and that their aim is mere sensible social democracy. If
so, then the sentence I quoted should also be welcomed by
them and by those they make cause with in the EU; I would, if
they all did so genuinely, gladly withdraw my detractions.
But when we look at the words and actions of this general and
dominant group in the EU it does not seem to tally with these
sentiments. Therefore I believe that a proposal for the UK to
join NAFTA will act as a litmus test of the true intentions of
the EU towards its future development. It ought to be
welcomed by an outward-looking liberal Europe; if it is not,
then it will reveal the ugly truth. Should the latter occur, then
the UK's bluff on Europe will have been well and truly called
also; we will have to choose, either to leave and renegotiate
some sort of arrangements for free trade and factor
movements, or to be absorbed into a new socialist republic of
Europe. In my remaining remarks I address the economic
factors (the political ones are quite obvious) that would affect
our choice.

The Balance Sheet Updated

About five years ago I wrote a paper which attempted to
calculate the net cost/benefit of our EU membership'[1], on the
assumption that it was all or nothing. Of course, in practice a
renegotiation would preserve many aspects of the relationship so such calculations are just a starting point. For what it
was worth, my sums indicated a rough 'even stevens' without
the Social Chapter/Charter or the euro; this rough balance
was made up of agriculture on the negative side and the

---

[1] Patrick Minford, *Britain and Europe: The Balance Sheet*, Centre for European
Studies and European Business Review: MCB University Press, 1996, p. 38.

Single Market together with our manufacturing inward investment (reducing unemployment) on the positive. Since then, however, there have been important developments. First, the projections I made then that the UK-EU trade balance in EU-protected manufacturing would turn positive have turned out to be wrong; instead the deficit remains of the order of 1% of UK GDP. Second, the UK has achieved more or less full employment, as the effects of labour market deregulation in the 1980s have worked through. Lastly we have had five more years of the Single Market and other EU regulation such as the Social Chapter, to which the UK has now signed up.   The costs identified with agriculture, the CAP and the UK's net budgetary contribution appear still to be broadly correct—at around 1.5% of GDP. In the earlier paper I suggested that reform might make these short-lived; but that judgement looks wrong.There is still no sign of serious reform of the CAP and it is realistic to project these costs into the foreseeable future.[2]

On manufacturing trade the changes imply that what was a net benefit has to be seen today as a net cost. In the earlier estimates the assumed positive balance gave a credit as did the assumption that many of those employed in manufacturing would have a low marginal product elsewhere or be unemployed. Now the trade deficit implies a net cost—of the order of 0.3-0.5% of GDP (say a 30-50% premium over world prices times net trade volume of 1% of GDP). Meanwhile the labour resources involved can be assumed to be transferable elsewhere at existing wages. This leaves the effects of the Single Market and other EU regulation, mainly of the labour market. For the latter I see no reason to revise my previous assessment that it remains a large threat to the essentially deregulated UK labour market; with such reregulation jobs and output would be lost on a major scale as

[2] Editor's Note: see 'Reforming the CAP', *Economic Affairs*, Vol. 20, No. 2, June 2000.

assumed then. With respect to the Single Market, estimates are still hard to make and generalisation is difficult. However the following statements seem appropriate pending the full surveys which we must hope will emerge:

1. instead of 'mutual recognition', Single Market regulation is tending to be 'harmonisation', usually at the highest not the lowest level of the 15 countries. This makes for excess regulation for a country like the UK where regulation has been light.

2. the EU's non-tariff barrier around manufacturing within the EU, given that we have a trade deficit in protected manufactures, acts against the UK interest compared with unilateral free trade at the unprotected world price. The reason is the same as for tariff barriers as above.

3. in services, the UK has a trade surplus and therefore should gain from the EU non-tariff customs union compared with unilateral free trade at the world price. However practical progress in creating the service customs union has been slow—the internal EU barriers remain substantial in aviation, financial products, public procurement, to name a few. In practice, the vested interests faced by governments in these areas are powerful and there may be little hope of progress. Hence the UK is not much better or worse off from this aspect of the 'Single Market'.

If one puts these elements together we have on the negative side a net cost on trade of some 2% of GDP, plus the threat from further regulation. If we leave on one side the issue of joining the euro where we have a clear opt-out, we are left with the Single Market where quantification at this stage is difficult but where scepticism of the benefits claimed (as for example in the Cecchini Report) is in order.

The Relevance to NAFTA

If the UK joined NAFTA it would effectively face world prices on manufactures and food, thus avoiding the 2% of

GDP costs involved on these. A NAFTA agreement with the UK on services would appear to be of little import either way given the limited progress on the service aspects of the Single Market. The most sensitive aspect would appear to be on visible trade.

It is then a matter of speculation whether the EU and the UK would on this visible trade reach a free trade agreement or would simply levy tariffs and non-tariff barriers on each other (mfn treatment). The EU might be willing to negotiate some sort of free trade/Single Market agreement with the UK in both manufactures and food, on the proviso that UK exports are not swollen by displacement from extra NAFTA production entering the UK. Under such an agreement the UK would obtain preferential EU prices on its EU exports while EU exporters to the UK would obtain only world prices. This would give a further gain to the UK. There is no terms of trade gain to the EU in such an agreement; with UK barriers their exports would have to go elsewhere to obtain world prices, without them they could get world prices in the UK. Nevertheless, they do gain from not having to divert their large exports in this way—a non-negligible one-off cost considering their very large exports to the UK. Either way the NAFTA membership would benefit the UK. From the US point of view the possible gains lie first in the market opportunities in the UK where prices and costs are higher than in the US; secondly in effecting a breach in the EU's trade barriers. The loss of the UK market would reduce substantially the gains to the continental EU from protection—thus the balance of interests within the EU could switch towards trade liberalisation. Thus the UK joining NAFTA could be the prelude to an eventual NAFTA-EU rapprochement.

Conclusion

A NAFTA-UK agreement would expose the UK market in visible trade to world market competition, a development that would be good for UK consumers and the UK taxpayer, to the tune of 2% of GDP. These gains would lead to a reduction of taxes and prices, stimulating growth and employment across the economy, but particularly in the rapidly-growing service sectors of the UK economy. One might reasonably assume that the EU would wish to negotiate a free trade agreement, with some safeguards, with the UK in order not to lose its access to one of its largest export markets; it would nevertheless in any case lose the gains it currently gets (of the order above) from the customs union arrangements on food and manufactures with the UK. As a result of the diminution of the customs union protection within the EU from the UK's departure, the EU's enthusiasm for protection may well diminish; so it is possible that a NAFTA-UK agreement could precipitate a general freeing of trade between the US and NAFTA on the one hand and the EU on the other. In the end I believe a UK-NAFTA rapprochement would be a force for good, not just for the UK for the detailed reasons given above, but also for the US which would derail the EU's growing protectionism, and ultimately and ironically for the EU itself which would gain immensely from this derailment. We might once again be able to contemplate, as some of us once did in the heyday of our Single Market hopes, the future of a free market Europe based on a loose, cooperative alliance of like-minded nations.

Commentary:
Could the United Kingdom Join a Global Free Trade Association?

Martin Howe QC

John Hulsman's challenging paper proposes that the United States and the United Kingdom, together with other pro-free trade nations, enter into a global Free Trade Association. The suggestion is not advanced as an alternative to the UK's existing membership of the European Union and participation in the EC's single market, but as complementing that membership.

Could the UK join the proposed global Free Trade Association, and at the same time retain its membership of the EU and the EC single market? Dr Hulsman correctly acknowledges that amendment of the existing European Treaties would be required in order for the UK to enter into bilateral trade arrangements with countries outside the EU. But what amendments would be needed, and could they work in practice? I propose to address this question first at a legal and technical level, before turning to the far less objective question of its political feasibility.

The UK's membership of the proposed global FTA impinges mainly on the structure of the European Community (EC) and the EC Treaty, otherwise known as the Treaty of Rome. Its relevance to the wider EU umbrella body and to the so-called 'inter-governmental pillars' of the Treaty on European Union (Maastricht Treaty) is more limited.

The fundamental point is that the EC is a customs union, as distinct from a free trade area. In principle, a country can belong at the same time to more than one free trade area. But in principle, it is not possible for a country to belong at the same time to two different customs unions. Nor can it belong to both a customs union and a free trade area, unless the customs union as a whole is within the free trade area.

This reason for this lies in the nature of a free trade area. A free trade area arrangement applies to trade between the countries who are members, but each member retains responsibility for its own external trade relations. It follows that the free trading rules apply only to goods which originate within the members of the free trade area. Otherwise, imports from third countries would pass into the member which had the lowest or zero external tariffs, and would then be re-exported to other countries within the free trade area. The member countries would then no longer be able to control their own trade relations with third countries.

In order to avoid this happening, customs checks need to be maintained between the members of the free trade area, and rules of origin are applied to discriminate between goods from outside the area and goods from within. Because of the need to combat avoidance devices, such as minor re-assembly operations on goods in substance manufactured outside the area, rules of origin tend to develop considerable complexity.

By contrast, a customs union does not need to apply rules of origin to goods which cross internal borders within the union. This is because goods from outside enter the union through a uniform external tariff and control régime, which (at least in theory) will be consistently applied by customs posts whatever country the goods enter through. Thus, it is possible within a customs union to dispense with routine customs checks on goods moving between member states, and this has been done within the EC since 1993.

It can therefore be seen that membership by the UK of the proposed FTA would involve significant adjustment of the EC Treaty, at least as regards its application to the UK. The UK would have to cease to be a member of the customs union, and customs controls involving the application of rules of origin would be applied to goods passing between the UK and other EC member states.

Although such changes would involve adjustment, they are certainly feasible in terms of drafting the necessary Treaty provisions and other legal rules. A model for such rules exists within the EAA Agreement,[1] which formed a free trade area between the EC single market and the then EFTA countries.[2] It provides for the 'four freedoms': free movement of goods,[3] and of persons, services and capital; however it applies only to products originating within the Area[4] and the EFTA members remain responsible for their own trade relations with third countries. The institutional arrangements of the EEA agreement are heavily unbalanced in favour of the EC;[5] however, it would not be necessary to copy across those institutional arrangements in order to lift out the rules needed to adapt the EC Treaty to provide a free trade area relationship, rather than a customs union, between the UK and the rest of the EC.

But a further and wider issue arises as a result of the nature of the EC single market construction exercise. The EC single market seeks to implement free trade in goods and services within the EC by means of the detailed harmonisation of all the relevant internal rules of the member states, relating to technical standards, the provision of services, intellectual

---

[1] 'Agreement on the European Economic Area', signed at Oporto on 2 May 1992.

[2] Except for Switzerland which stayed outside and continued on its own, looser, free trade agreement with the EC.

[3] Except for the agricultural and fisheries sectors, which are excluded from the Agreement: Article 8(3).

[4] Article 8(2). The rules of origin are set out in Protocol 4 to the Agreement; these rules, together with their detailed Appendices, extend to 132 pages.

[5] For example, Article 102 provides for the EFTA members to adapt their laws to follow new EC Directives in order to guarantee 'the homogeneity' of the EEA; and Article 111 pressurises, if not actually compels, the EFTA countries to follow the interpretations of the European Court of Justice on corresponding EC rules.

property and an ever widening circle of other provisions.[6] From a bureaucratic point of view this process leads to a theoretical ideal in which goods and services can be traded on a perfectly level playing field under identical conditions throughout the EC.

However, the harmonisation approach has a serious drawback from a practical point of view. It leads to over-regulation and over-elaboration of rules. Every member state is reluctant to see dilution of its existing standards in the jointly adopted rules, and as a result there is a strong tendency for existing national regulations to be cumulated. The resulting EC measures have a strong tendency towards excessive stringency, excessive inspection régimes, and excessive bureaucracy and paperwork.[7]

The problem with these elaborate EC single market rules is that they not only act as the minimum standards for trade between member states, but also the member states must apply them internally as well.[8] Therefore for example, the

---

[6] For example, a report prepared for the European Commission (Storme Report, 'Approximation of Judiciary Law in the European Union', Kluwer) has recommended that the rules of the civil courts should be harmonised because divergences between such rules could affect traders who sell goods or services across borders within the EC.

[7] This point could be made good with numerous examples. One example which illustrates the point is Council Regulation (EC) No. 2200/96 of 28 October 1996 on the common organisation of the market in fruit and vegetables. This lays down a series of quality standards applicable to every individual type of fruit and vegetable on the market; those standards specify, for example, minimum and maximum sizes for each type of fruit, Commission Regulation (EC) No. 2257/94 of 16 September 1994 laying down quality standards for bananas and Annex I, Section II even requiring that bananas shall be free from 'abnormal curvature'. An elaborate EC-wide system of inspection and required documentation is set up to enforce the standards all the way from producer to customer.

[8] As held for example by the ECJ in *R. v. Licensing Authority of the Dept of Health, ex parte Scotia Pharmaceuticals Ltd* Case C-440/93 [1995] ECR 1-2851: the member states must comply strictly with the terms of the harmonisation Directive applying to pharmaceutical products and are simply not free to issue authorisations outside the terms of the Directive, even if completely satisfied that no danger to human health would result.

price paid by British financial institutions in return for the possible benefits of being allowed to sell their services directly into other member states is compliance with onerous EC rules relating to, amongst other matters, capital adequacy. And this price is paid by all British financial institutions, whether or not they are ever likely to do any business with the Continent.

The EC requirement of widespread harmonisation of internal rules leads to a potential conflict with UK membership of the proposed global FTA. The UK's obligations under the FTA, either directly or in consequence of its disputes procedure, might be to dismantle or simplify over-elaborate technical standards or over restrictive rules relating to the provision of services. However, if those rules originate from EC regulations or directives, then the UK would be obliged under EC law to continue to apply the EC rules internally.

Of course, such a potential for conflict already exists between EC rules and the rules of the WTO and other free trade agreements to which the EC as a whole belongs. The difference is that the EC can collectively change its rules to comply, but the UK could not, as the EC Treaty at present stands, comply with its obligations under the FTA when called upon to do so. And since the ethos of the global FTA is to be more pro free-trade than existing global institutions, the likelihood of conflict between its rules and the rules imposed upon the UK by the EC is increased.

For UK membership of the global FTA to work, a further change to the EC Treaty would be needed. That would be to allow the UK to relax EC harmonised rules, at least when required to do so by FTA rules, in the case of goods and services within the UK market. This would make sense in free trade terms. UK exporters to the rest of the EC would still need to comply with the full EC rules, but would only have to comply with the relaxed rules when selling goods and services domestically within the UK; and the same relaxed rules would apply to goods or services imported from other members of the FTA. So long as exporters from other EC states were also given the option if they chose to comply with the relaxed, rather than full, rules on exports into the UK, then the principle of non-discrimination within the EC market would be upheld.

Such a situation would of course be anathema to single market purists, since there would be a zone (the UK) in which goods or services could be traded without the same restrictions as are applicable to the rest of the EC market. However, the more this concept is considered, the more intrinsically desirable it appears, quite apart from its relevance to the possible adhesion of the UK to a global FTA. The right to derogate from EC rules in the case of internally traded goods and services, and goods and services imported from non-EC countries, would be a welcome antidote to the present one-way street under which EC-imposed technical standards and trading rules become more and more barnacle encrusted and elaborate. The existing EC standards would continue to have value as providing a 'passport' which, if complied with, would lead to freedom to trade throughout the EC market. But the provision of goods and services on the UK market under more relaxed and less cumbersome rules would provide welcome economic pressure to reduce unnecessary regulatory burdens.

So far, the conclusion can be reached that it would be feasible at a legal and practical trading level to amend the EC Treaty to permit the UK to join the proposed global FTA. The minimum changes required would be (1) to exclude the UK from the Common Customs Tariff and the common commercial policy,[9] and to restrict the application of the Treaty rules on free movement of goods[10] on UK/EC trade to goods

---

[9] EC Treaty, Articles 25 and 131-4.

[10] EC Treaty, Articles 25 and 28-31.

originating within the UK or EC respectively;[11] and (2) to permit the UK to derogate from EC single market rules in relation to internally traded goods and services, at least where necessary to comply with its obligations under the FTA. Again at a legal and technical level, these changes to the Treaty could be made, leaving the UK as a full participating member of the EC and EU in all other respects. These arrangements would be similar in structure to the UK's existing 'opt-out' from the third stage of EMU.[12]

Those would be the minimum changes that would be necessary. There is an argument that more extensive changes would be desirable. For example, the continued imposition of EC employment and workplace laws on businesses within the UK is not logically necessary or justified by access to the EC single market, except on the basis of 'handicap thy neighbour' arguments which lead on to calls for a worldwide 'Social GATT'.[13] In a free trade area relationship with the United States, the UK would wish to have the freedom to adapt its employment and workplace laws to ensure a standard of competitiveness comparable to that in the USA market.

There are therefore arguments in favour of a more extensive loosening of the relationship between the EC and the UK, whilst retaining the free access to the EC single market. The recent conclusion of the EC-Mexico Free Trade Agreement illustrates that it is possible for a country to enjoy

---

[11] It would also be possible to exclude the UK from most or all of the provisions on indirect tax harmonisation (Article 93 and the VAT directives made under that Article). This would not be necessary in order for the UK to join the global FTA, but the justification for more harmonisation of indirect taxes would disappear because customs controls would involve VAT refund on export, and VAT and excise taxation on importation, on goods crossing the UK/EC border.

[12] Set out in Protocol No. 25 to the EC treaty, adopted at Maastricht.

[13] See for example European Commission Forward Studies Unit, 'Globalization and Social Governance in Europe and the United States', Working Paper, 1999.

a looser relationship with the EC which gives its exporters virtually the same access to the EC market for goods and services as that enjoyed by EC members, but without many of the economic and political costs. The example of Mexico is of particular interest, because of course it is already in a free trade relationship with the United States via its membership of NAFTA.

So far, this assessment has dealt with what would be feasible at a legal and technical level, rather than with feasibility at a political level. The changes set out above would collide at a political level with some articles of faith which are deeply embedded within the European institutions. The first is the concept of the *acquis Communautaire*: the idea that what the Community has, it holds; that it must never abandon or reduce any of its competences and that it is destined forever to expand the scope of its powers. The second is the concept of market harmonisation: not only that intra-EC trade must be free of restrictions, but that it must be conducted under perfectly uniform conditions across the whole EC market: a cost or restriction on one must therefore be made to apply to all. The third is the concept that the EC/EU is about forging a political union and that free trade is merely a means to that end;[14] for a member to get the benefit of the free trade but to escape the political bonds is unacceptable from this perspective.

---

[14] As the European Court expressed it in *Re Draft Treaty on a European Economic Area:* Opinion 1/91 [1992] 1 CMLR 245: 'The Rome Treaty aims to achieve economic integration leading to the establishment of an internal market and economic and monetary union. Article 1 of the Single European Act makes it clear that the objective of all the Community treaties is to contribute together to making concrete progress towards European unity. It follows from the foregoing that the provisions of the Rome Treaty on free movement and competition, far from being an end in themselves, are only means of attaining those objectives. . . . As the Court of Justice has consistently held, the Community treaties established a new legal order for the benefit of which the States have limited their sovereign rights, *in ever wider fields*, and the subjects of which comprise not only the member-States but also their nationals.' (Emphasis added.)

Policy analysts viewing Europe from the perspective of Washington may find it difficult to appreciate the depth to which these concepts are entrenched within the culture of the institutions of the European Union, or the scale of the clash which a challenge to these concepts within the EU will provoke. Nevertheless, there are reasons quite apart from this global FTA proposal which mean that the UK will need to challenge these concepts in any case. If the UK wishes to remain an independent nation state for the long term future and to remain economically competitive, it is essential that the EU should be turned away from the mindset represented by these concepts, or at least that the EU's structure should be made flexible enough to allow non-integrationist states such as the UK no longer to be subject to the rigid application of those principles.

Viewed in the wider context of the argument that the future of Europe lies in a flexible, open, free trade model, Dr Hulsman's proposal would represent an additional incentive for challenging these EU super-Statist concepts. The recovery of the UK's right to conduct its bilateral trade relations can be viewed as an important goal in making the structure of the EU more open and flexible. The global FTA, or some other link with the USA or NAFTA, would be one of many possibilities that would then be opened up in the conduct of the UK's global trade relations.

Commentary:
Enlargement of NAFTA:
West is Best, but East Comes First?
David Davis MP

Any practising politician has to answer three questions about John Hulsman's excellent paper. First, does this proposal offer real benefits? Second, can it be done? Third, is there any better way to deliver the same or better outcome?

There is little doubt that, of itself a free trade zone that encompassed Britain and the current NAFTA countries would be beneficial to all involved. However, such a proposal cannot exist as it stands, because the UK has given up its ability to decide its own external trade policy as a part of its continuing membership of the European Union.

This is where all of the practical difficulty of the Hulsman proposal lies. For some it is also where its attraction lies, in the prospect of the UK having an alternative to the European Union, one that may credibly offer a better economic future, with larger markets and fewer challenges to national sovereignty. The coexistence between EU and NAFTA membership that John Hulsman talks of is not a legal or political possibility at the moment. Many of the supporters of the Hulsman idea, although not John Hulsman himself, are supporters largely because it seems to offer an easier exit route from the EU.

That is frankly not in prospect in the foreseeable future. Ignoring the merits or demerits of the exercise, it is certainly not going to happen under a Labour government. It would only happen under a highly Euro-sceptical Tory government, operating with a high degree of unanimity and/or with a very large majority. Given the propensity for referendums these days, it would also require a high degree of popular antagonism to the European Union. This quartet of conditions is unlikely to be met in less than two Parliaments, if ever.

So we are considering a timetable of at least ten years. This brings us to whether there exists a better alternative policy for the American government, viewed from the American, the British, and indeed the overall Western democratic capitalist interest. In my view there is.

Before I elaborate the detailed alternative, I should explain that I have for some years held the view that the West has for too long pursued too defensive a foreign policy. For fifty years Soviet promotion of Communism abroad has led the West, and America in particular, to operate on the basis of alliances and spheres of interest dictated by national strategic interest and Kissinger style *realpolitik*. The policy was not greatly successful. The opposition today is not the Soviet bloc, but an inchoate mix of problems driven by ethnic conflict and the battle for resources, by nationalism and poverty, an inflammable mix made worse by dictatorship, repression, and economic failure.

The answer to this is a foreign policy that favours those countries that make the political choices that will help them save themselves. We—America and the rest of the West—should operate a freedom-based foreign policy. Instead of throwing bribes at repressive governments under the label of foreign aid, we should favour the democracies that allow proper human freedoms, under the rule of law, particularly the freedom to own property and trade. These are the individual freedoms that set whole nations free of poverty and oppression. This assistance should consist largely of opening up our markets to such countries, rewarding domestic freedom with international free trade.

This rather general policy has an immediate, not to say urgent, application in today's European politics. The old Warsaw Pact countries all stand today at a crossroads. Down one route there is the Russian model—weak democratic and legal structures, and a corrupt and crime-ridden economy. Down the other route is the Czech model, with reasonably strong democratic and legal institutions, and a vigorous, effective, and largely honest economy. Every old Soviet-style economy faces this choice today, and the route they take will determine the future of Central Europe, and as a direct result will influence the security of all of Europe.

The new democracies are still poor, with GDP/capita between about $4,000 and $11,000. Their economies are still fragile, with growth rates that vary between a crushing minus 7% and a soaring plus 7%. It is no coincidence that the weakest performers tend to be the least democratic, the least free, and to have the most problems with corrupt institutions. Central Europe is populated with a range of countries that have the potential either to be great successes, or to be Russias in miniature. Their potential for economic success is very real. Their costs are low, but their skills are not. The educational standards in these ex-communist countries are very high, given the relative poverty of the countries. The eighth grade science achievements survey in 1995 showed the Czech Republic second in the world behind Singapore, Bulgaria 5th, Slovenia 7th, and Hungary 9th, all ahead of supposedly technologically capable countries like Britain and America. Mathematics is a similar story. The poverty inflicted on them by nearly half a century of Communism should make them hungry for success—a hunger stimulated by the visible fruits of that success just across the Western borders. Their institutions and legal systems are weak, but improving. Some of their politicians understand the importance of property rights and strong legal systems in a market economy, and this is being helped by some of the Western aid and advice that they are receiving. They have most of the ingredients of real success.

Quite reasonably they look to their nearest neighbour, the European Union, to help them make the transition. But by far the most important missing component of their growth strategy is access to markets. The keystone of that strategy must be free trade. And the EU is explicitly not providing that. There a yawning chasm between the rhetoric and the reality of EU trade policy. A great deal is said in the public pronouncements of the EU about the importance of free trade. But the reality of the domestic politics of the EU is that its performance almost never lives up to the promise. The protectionist instinct always seems to win out. It is not much of an exaggeration to describe the EU's policy towards the new democracies as 'zero tariffs on what they do not make and high tariffs on what they do.'

As a result the new democracies are condemned to run balance of trade deficits with their supposed saviour, the European Union. Thus Poland's trade deficit with the EU doubled from 3.04 billion ECU in 1995 to 7.6 billion in 1996. Today we see Poland involved in a virtual trade war with Germany.

It will be little better when they get into the EU. Access to European markets is likely to be bought at a crippling price. Driven by fear of the low cost competition from east of the old Iron Curtain for their traditional industries, the Europeans are doing anything but making it easy for the new democracies. The European Union is insisting that the new applicants for Union membership shoulder the huge burden of existing European legislation. This weight of environmental, health, safety and labour legislation is enormous. It will absorb 3% or 4% of its economy every year for several years.

Such a burden would stop Poland's growth dead. It would shatter its ability to compete at precisely the moment Poland was hoping to exploit its new European markets. It would distract the efforts of all Poland's best business managers away from meeting the demands of the market to meeting the demands of the bureaucrats, precisely at the time they need to focus exclusively on market opportunities. And what is true for Poland is also true for the Czechs, for the Hungarians, for all of the new democracies.

So the gold at the end of the European rainbow for the new democracies will be fool's gold. Instead of new markets delivering jobs and prosperity, their industries will face new burdens and new competition simultaneously, delivering unemployment and despair. Europe is likely to fail the new democracies. This is why America should be looking to enlarge NAFTA first to those countries for whom free trade is a lifeline, not just a luxury.

Enlargement of NAFTA to include the new democracies of Central and Eastern Europe would strike an enormous blow for freedom, democracy and stability, would enlarge the world economy, and would be an imaginative act of enlightened self interest for the USA. Free trade for the new democracies would make the difference between the agonised struggle with inflation, with collapsing industries, with unemployment, with poverty and with corruption, which mark some of the old Warsaw Pact countries, and the alternative future of the new European tiger economies. A number of them already have most of the capabilities, given the market opportunity, to grow at the critical 7% rate that doubles the size of their economies every decade. The Czechs, the Poles, the Hungarians, the Lithuanians, the Slovenians, only need that opportunity. Others still have work to do, but they will undoubtedly emulate dramatic success when it happens.

If the American government were imaginative enough to take this step, the new democracies would be extremely likely to take them up on their offer. Joining the European Union is no longer a popular as it was, now the realities are sinking in. It was always more a badge of membership of the free world than a carefully considered strategy to many of the escapees from the Warsaw Pact. For these purposes, NAFTA is just as good, with more benefits and fewer costs.

So the possibility of bringing the Central Europeans into an American-led free trade area has massive direct benefits for democracy, stability and prosperity, but it also has large indirect benefits too. It is likely to change the whole climate of negotiation with Europe. Such a strategy might prove the key to unlocking an advance in world economic freedom that has a greater impact than the current clumsy efforts of the WTO.

Being in NAFTA (or the Free World Free Trade Area, as it would be better known by then) would radically enhance the negotiating position of the new democracies with respect to Europe, if they still wanted to join. The European Union, on the other hand would find itself surrounded by a free trade zone that would force it to face up to its own fatal flaws. Suddenly the attractions to, say, Siemens, to invest in low-cost, low regulation, high growth Poland, would be even greater than they are now. Germany would find itself with a massive incentive to deregulate and compete. And what Germany wants, Europe eventually delivers.

Which brings us back to the position of Britain. The negotiating position of the British government in these circumstances would be dramatically improved. With the borders of Europe that much more porous, with the countries outside the EU borders becoming the new tiger economies, doubling in size every decade, the virtues of economic freedom would be very obvious to the people of the European Union.

If Britain were offered NAFTA membership under these circumstances, the European Union would have to take it seriously. Many others would be seeking joint membership at the same time, but on terms set by the peoples of Europe, not by the bureaucrats of Brussels. The Scandinavian EU members would have some interesting questions to answer, bracketed as they would be between the Baltic States and Norway, all potentially in NAFTA. Similarly Austria would face some bracing competition, placed as it is between

Switzerland and the Czech Republic, again both immediate NAFTA candidates. Suddenly the multi-speed option would be a reality, with each country able to decide exactly how much sovereignty it wanted to give up in exchange for partial or total EU membership. And it would be quite clear that the 'high speed' states would be those in the outer rim of Europe, not the sclerotic inner core.

The key to such a strategy is America. No other country has the economic and political power and self-confidence to attempt it. Despite the fact that its main thrust is European, no other country would stand to gain so much by doing it. Its thrust is based upon ideas which epitomise all the things that America stands for, and in carrying it through America would achieve as lasting a transformation of Eastern Europe as the Marshall plan did for the West some half century ago.

Commentary:
Hulsman: The Other Side of Barmy
Bill Jamieson

Hooray for Robin Cook. Days ahead of a visit to London by US Senator Phil Gramm in summer 2000, he pronounced the idea of British membership of the North American Free Trade Agreement (NAFTA) as 'barmy'. That his remarks also coincided with a visit of senior American businessmen to the UK organised by the Treasury and the Department of Trade & Industry added to the levity.

The Foreign Secretary's curt dismissal had several unintended consequences. First, it ensured more media attention for Senator Gramm's visit than would otherwise have been the case. It also revealed the Euro-fixation of this administration, Cook's fixation in particular, and the extent to which Labour has adopted the continental world-view. Long gone is the vision of a previous Labour Foreign Secretary Ernest Bevin, who saw the UK at the critical juncture of three overlapping circles: Europe, America and the Commonwealth.

It also revealed the existence of a highly critical Foreign and Commonwealth Office memorandum on the NAFTA idea. Finally, though rather more disturbingly for proponents of a UK-NAFTA link, it revealed the height of the mountain to be climbed for this idea to gain wider acceptance.

Membership of NAFTA is often advocated by those who see in it a means of disarming public concern about an 'isolated' Britain were she to reject further convergence with the EU. This presupposes that there is a wider public support for membership of NAFTA than there is for 'Euro-scepticism' in the broad sense. Yet, far from Euro-scepticism

51

being a sub-specie of support for a free trade pact with North America, the opposite is the case: membership of NAFTA is the sub-specie of Euro-scepticism. Not all Euro-sceptics are in favour of a NAFTA tie-up.

Now why should this be? Why is there not a much greater embrace by the British of closer links with the US, based on the long affinity of which Dr. John Hulsman writes so eloquently in his paper? And why are so many, not just the Foreign Secretary, quick to denounce the notion as 'barmy'?

Thanks to Hulsman, Senator Phil Gramm and others, the full extent of Britain and America's trading and investment links is now more widely appreciated. And the more that is so, the more compelling the idea of a UK-North American free trade pact becomes. It is also being borne on the in-tide of globalisation and the relentless rise of e-commerce and e-business which works to reduce distance as a barrier to marketing and trade.

But while there is a potent economic case, growing in strength with changes in the world economy, the notion of stronger affinity through a trade tie-up is more problematic. Some, I fear, are too polite to point out the difficulties. In Dr. Hulsman's case I do sense a rush of historical romanticism has caused him to overlook both the role of the US in pushing Britain further into the EU, and the political and constitutional difficulties of extrication.

Hulsman takes as given a widespread political support in Britain and the US for membership of NAFTA, drawing, as he sets out, on common bonds of language, history, culture and mutuality of interest in trade and investment. 'It is no exaggeration to say', he writes,

'that America has no more proven or dependable an ally than Great Britain. History has underscored the commonalities of the relationship with ties built on common language, common history and common culture.' (p. 9)

Britain's entry into a global Free Trade Association (FTA) would require it, he writes,

> 'to shift its politico-economic focus from Europe and instead return its gaze to what is clearly the most successful partnership of the twentieth century – the special relationship between the UK of Cornwallis and the US of Hamilton and Washington.' (p. 11)

Ronald Reagan could hardly have put it better. But rhetorically pleasing though all this is, it is too misty-eyed. It ignores the need for a transformation in geo-political outlook in Washington every bit as radical as that required in the UK for the idea to gain momentum. For Hulsman's analysis makes light of a quite different, and more uncomfortable historical truth: the powerful role played by successive US administrations, first, in pushing Britain into the original 'Common Market', and second in cajoling Britain down the road of European convergence at every possible opportunity. That Phil Gramm, a widely respected US senator, should urge on Britain closer trading links with North America as a means of avoiding the alternative fate of EU integration is not without a certain piquancy. It is largely because of American pressure that Britain is so deeply involved in the EU and, as a result, has lost control of her external trade policy that would permit her to join NAFTA now.

American foreign policy since the 1950s had as one of its key strategic objectives in Europe the full integration of the UK into 'ever closer union'. There has not been, as Hulsman writes, 'the most successful partnership of the Twentieth Century', but rather an all too evident and insistent desire, first, to reduce Britain's independent global role, and second to subsume the UK into European economic and monetary union on the perception that this would best further US interests. Most of us recall that haunting observation of Dean Acheson, the urbane and liberal former US Secretary of State, that 'Great Britain has lost an empire and has not yet found a role.' But few recall what Acheson went on immediately to add:

'The attempt to play a separate power role, that is, a role apart from Europe, a role based on a 'special relationship' with the United States. . . — this role is about played out.'[1]

Acheson was particularly scathing about the Commonwealth, Britain's third circle of influence, and his criticism flowed from a basic assumption of American foreign policy in the immediate post-war years that the British preference system should be ended. It was the constant assault on this that propelled Britain to look more favourably on the shared tariff system of the Common Market. Moreover, the over-riding obsession for the US at this time was a belief in a US-friendly hegemony in Western Europe in order to counter the real threat of Soviet expansionism. Post war US foreign policy was shaped by three powerful Secretaries of State—Dean Acheson, John Foster Dulles and George Ball—and they shared a visceral dislike of Britain's commonwealth arrangements and a wish to solidify Western Europe into one pro-American political bloc. Suez (1956) and the brutality of America's financial sanction on Britain left a bitter aftertaste with many in the UK. American policy was driven by quite different imperatives. In the words of Douglas Evans, who so tellingly chronicled how Britain came to be in the Common Market:

'they were more interested in winning the immediate arguments than questioning whether their assumptions— about the means of building a permanent alliance community to resist the Soviet threat—were correct ones. Secondly, as

[1] Quoted in Douglas Evans, *While Britain Slept: The Selling of the Common Market*, London: Victor Gollancz, 1975, p. 123.

non-elected officials, they had little or no feel for the democratic process in either the United States or Europe. Unsurprisingly they were not too choosy over whether the European comity they were to foster would be a democratic one. Third, in the pursuit of American national security, a legitimate interest inextricably bound up with Western Europe's own survival, America's chief foreign policy architects failed to see the irony that in the process of safeguarding America's national sovereignty they were urging the Europeans to surrender theirs in a federal system of some sort.'[2]

This was the background to President Kennedy's encouragement to Macmillan to apply for membership of the Common Market, and for subsequent substantial American support—political and financial—for a Yes vote in the 1975 referendum. And all this has to be acknowledged because these basic instincts of the White House and the US foreign policy machine are still broadly intact today: encouragement of UK convergence with the EU as a means of neutralising the visceral anti-Americanism of France, and to encourage EU convergence as a means of promoting greater European burden-sharing on defence and security.

This broad impulse to support convergence is shared by the large American corporations, investment banks and bond trading houses such as Salomon, Merrill Lynch and Goldman Sachs, those powerful out-riders of America's global interests. On issues such as British membership of the single currency and even the creation of a single European bourse, the US banks are in favour, and tend to regard British concerns and hesitations as minor and irrelevant irritants that can be swept aside. Indeed, with the current Washington administration there is little evidence of the 'special relationship' of which Hulsman writes: left to the Clinton

---

[2] Douglas Evans, *op. cit.*, p. 129.

White House alone, Britain would have been rolled up long ago into the European project and would by now have lost her currency.

It is for these reasons that many older voters in Britain are wary of talk of shared political ideals and goals with the US, while among younger voters there is a potent dislike for the homogenisation of tastes that US corporations have come to represent. The British voter who does not much care for European integration is often the same voter who suspects that globalisation will do for UK institutions just the same. There has to be greater evidence than now pertains that in Washington the UK is something more than part of the general converging blur that is Europe, that she has interests different, and distinct from, those of the continental economies.

Dr. Hulsman also has an over-simplified notion of the UK's freedom to join or not to join external free trade alliances. This was effectively signed away by the 1972 European Communities Act, and, because the EU is a customs union not a free trade area, all members must sign up for NAFTA or none. The idea of the Jospin government agreeing to membership of NAFTA is, to put it no stronger, romantic, and no serious consideration can be given by Britain to this question unless she is prepared to undergo a radical recalibration of her membership of the EU.[3]

There are many who believe that this has all come too late, that the die is cast and that the best the Euro-sceptic movement can do is to 'delay the inevitable.' Yet the power of Hulsman's paper is its challenge to accepted Foreign Office notions of inevitability. That there is a potent mutuality of economic interest between the UK and the countries of NAFTA is now in little doubt. British direct investment in the United States in 1997 stood at $18.3 billion, greater than that

---

[3] For a fuller discussion, see Bill Jamieson and Patrick Minford, *Britain and Europe: Choices for Change*, London: Politeia, 1999, chapters 7, 8 and 9.

of any other country and accounting for some 30 per cent of the total of all foreign direct investment in the US.

This pattern of heavy UK investment in the US has continued, so that last year 60 per cent of funds invested overseas by UK institutions went into the US, compared with 31 per cent in the other 14 EU countries.

Taking overall UK investment (foreign direct investment plus portfolio investment plus UK bank lending) there is a huge commitment to the NAFTA countries, and investments in these economies now earn for Britain in excess of £26.7 billion a year, or 24 per cent of all the UK's overseas investment income.[4]

The remarkable vibrant performance of the US economy in recent years compared to the continental EU economies should also make policymakers think twice before repeating the epithet of 'barmy' to a NAFTA/UK tie-up. I am grateful to Keith Marsden, the Geneva-based economist, for the following: NAFTA has 38 per cent more consumers than the economies of the 11 country European single currency zone, and these consumers are 20 per cent better off in terms of GDP per head.

The NAFTA economies have been growing at twice the rate of those in Euroland: NAFTA has an average GDP growth rate of 3.6 per cent over the last seven years, compared with only 1.8 per cent in Euroland.

NAFTA has a better employment record than Euroland. Since 1992 the number of jobs has risen by 38 per cent in Mexico and 13 per cent in both Canada and the US. In Euroland, the equivalent figure is just 3 per cent.

Workers in NAFTA countries earn more and are taxed less than those in Euroland. A single worker with no children on an average production wage has a net income of $20,388 in the US—compared to just $16,577 in Germany.

NAFTA countries are more attractive to external investors

---

[4] See *UK Balance of Payments Pink Book*, 1999, Office of National Statistics.

than Euroland countries. In 1998 the value of foreign direct investment into NAFTA countries was $229 billion, compared to $140 billion in Euroland.[5]

From a US standpoint, greater recognition of the lower tax regime and lighter regulatory climate in Britain is vital if US companies invested in Britain are not to suffer from the full brunt of EU fiscal and regulatory harmonisation. America has more invested in the UK than any other external country—$22.4 billion, or 20 per cent of the total of all US foreign direct investment. The US has thus a great deal to defend and much to lose if the UK simply caves in to the intensifying convergence pressure.

In this, Hulsman's paper is both an inspiration as to why this proposal should be much higher up the UK policy agenda than it is, and a warning that such an elevation will require an almighty struggle with the *status quo*—on both sides of the Atlantic.

---

[5] Keith Marsden, *Towards 'A Treaty of Commerce': Euroland and NAFTA Compared*, Centre for Policy Studies, July 2000.

Response:
The End of the Beginning
John C. Hulsman

Churchill, speaking at the Lord Mayor's Day Luncheon, November 10, 1942, was asked to comment on the war effort. He responded by saying, 'Now this is not the end. It is not even the beginning of the end. But it is the end of the beginning'. I think nothing so aptly sums up the current British grappling with their relationship with Europe, and more broadly, their place in the world in the post-Cold War era.

When Dr. Gerald P. O'Driscoll Jr. and I responded to the kind invitation of the Institute of Economic Affairs to deliver remarks on the possible politico-economic alternatives to British entry into the euro, we were well aware we would be discussing the most important issue to confront the UK since the war. We were also aware that a very odd veil of silence had descended on what should have been a ferocious debate about Britain's place in the world. As one Tory MP told me at the IEA meeting where I presented my paper, 'Many of us agree with your prescriptions, but the time is not right for saying so.' It occurred to us, that given that attitude, the debate, such as it was, had grown very stale. It seemed to us that anyone questioning the Blair line on Europe was somehow (to borrow Robin Cook's wonderful phrase) 'barmy', that it was seen as downright odd to look for alternatives to Britain being subsumed into Europe. Such a position could only lead to the UK adopting its standard psychological position regarding ever-closer European integration: we do not like it, but as there are no alternatives, we had better sign up and try to keep the process within reason.

But there *are* alternatives and we were determined to prove this. The speech I gave confirmed that there is a real appetite in the UK to explore all the options Britain has before it. Only from this position of intellectual and political strength can the UK make a genuine, informed decision where and with whom it wishes to cast its lot.

Fortunately, the facts against Britain being wholly subsumed into a centralised, anti-democratic, protectionist Europe were squarely on our side. As Patrick Minford points out, perhaps the key phrase in my text is the challenge I throw down to all those soothing voices claiming that continental EU leaders do not really mean what they say about the nature of Brussels. The EU should welcome British desires to form a closer trading link with the US if its nature is genuinely pro-American and pro-free trade. This should be the litmus test regarding divining the nature of the EU's intentions. I have learned from long experience that European leaders, even more than most politicians, should be judged above all by their actions, and not their rhetoric. Beyond rightly seizing on this critical point, Professor Minford decisively illustrates that economically the EU is simply not a very good deal for Britain, with a net cost on trade being 2% of GDP, plus the all-too-real threat of further regulation. Analysis of this calibre begs the question: if all is not well with the European economic experiment, perhaps the option of forging closer ties with the US should be explored in far greater detail.

Martin Howe decisively proves that legally Britain can join a Free Trade Association with the US. He expertly weaves his way through the legal thicket, directly confronting what Jerry and I have called 'the customs union argument'. How can Britain negotiate to join an FTA with the US when it has ceded its power to negotiate such arguments to Brussels?

The straightforward answer is that the UK will have to recalibrate legally its trading regime with the EU, something that Mr. Howe points out, it should do anyway. By joining the European Economic Area, it would be possible for a country to enjoy a looser relationship with the EU that gives its exporters virtually the same access to the EU market for goods and services as that enjoyed by the other EU members, but without many of the political and economic costs. The example of the recent EU-Mexico free trade agreement provides a precedent for such action.

Mr. Howe goes on to provide, in the clear and precise style that only a first-rate lawyer can muster, many of the details as to how this process would work, looking at the actual agreements made between the various states comprising the EU. As the devil is always in the detail for Brussels, Mr. Howe does the US-UK cause a great service in this respect. In order to participate in both a EU-led trading bloc and a Free Trade Association (FTA) with the US, the UK would need to relax its EU harmonised rules in the case of goods and services (which are almost always statist) when required to do so by the FTA. Being able to derogate from EU rules in the case of internally traded goods and services and goods and services imported from non-EU countries would be similar to obtaining an opt-out. Such a policy would strengthen efforts to make the future architecture of the continent resemble a Europe *a la carte*, in which beyond accepting that certain minimal basic commonalities must be met by the members of Europe's critical multilateral organisations, individual countries must be free to pick and choose what elements of the European experiment they wish to join.

As Mr. Howe rightly notes, such an approach is at odds with the EU's notion of constantly expanding its competencies, as it sees itself destined forever to increase the scope of its powers. This entrenched concept will need to be politically overcome. But again, Mr. Howe is right in saying that this should be done anyway.

I would like to provoke Mr. Howe a little further by presenting him with an additional legal argument that is currently making the rounds in Washington about 'the customs union problem'. Senator Phil Gramm has observed that two provisions of the Treaty of Rome limiting Britain's ability to enter into other trade expansion agreements (such as an FTA arrangement with the US) violate the General Agreements on Tariffs and Trade (GATT) rules. GATT trade ministers said in 1994 that, 'A regional arrangement must facilitate trade among its members, and not raise trade barriers between its members and other nations.' Surely the EU has not met this requirement (the Common Agricultural Policy leaps to mind). It would seem that the European Union is undermining the letter and spirit of the GATT, and must therefore modify Treaty of Rome articles 133 and 310 which limit the sovereign powers of its members to negotiate trade agreements with countries out of the EU, as they are inconsistent with Article 24 of the GATT. If this is so, 'the customs union problem,' part of the mortar around the protectionist EU wall, ought to come down with a crash.

David Davis, MP, long a leader in this struggle, offers in his critique practical political reasoning combined with a rare mastery of the subject. However, I think that his 10-year prognosis for developing the right political climate in the UK to have a government that is receptive to an FTA offer from the US is excessive. At some point, Prime Minister Blair is going to have to put his premiership on the line in a euro-referendum, a contest where he ought to be beaten, given the overwhelming and sustained evidence of the opinion polls. Following such a defeat, the UK joining an FTA with the US becomes a very viable alternative, either under a weakened (and presumably chastened) Labour Party or under a reinvigorated Tory government.

I favour free trade by any means. As such, I would welcome the UK being asked to join NAFTA as Mr. Davis proposes. Several of my American colleagues who are sceptical about the UK joining the euro favour just such an approach. It is not that I am against this, I just do not believe it will work politically in the US. Currrently in the US, NAFTA is (wrongly) viewed in an unfavourable light. The establishment of NAFTA was such a fraught process that there are examples of congressmen on both sides of the aisle who lost their jobs over this one issue. There is a misplaced public conception that banding together with Mexico and Canada has led to the loss of American jobs, so an extension of this unpopular agreement is unlikely to find support within the government (witness Chile's futile attempts to join NAFTA). Blessed with a far more vigorous economy than Mexico's, Chile has all but given up on NAFTA accession after waiting years to join. The politics of NAFTA accession are simply toxic.

There are also certain conceptual advantages to the FTA over the NAFTA route. The FTA is a voluntary and inclusive association whose membership is based solely on a policy commitment by its member states to a genuinely liberal global trading order. My plan embraces a fundamental commitment to a state's sovereignty. Its economic policies and the choices they represent will determine whether or not a country qualifies for the grouping. The numerical target that determines membership in the FTA allows for self-selection, giving the whole project an inclusivity the NAFTA alternative lacks. Advocates for the FTA want to form an association with countries that share a common politico-economic culture pertaining to trade. States select themselves, based on their economic decisions—the process is not an example of American fiat. The FTA will not be a US-dominated structure in which a member country must either agree to American policies or be excluded from joining. Unlike the NAFTA proposal, it is neither Euro-centric nor dominated by American desires. This global rather than regional approach is much more in accord with the modern global marketplace and the 'death of distance' characteristic that defines it. These facts can only increase its attractiveness around the globe.

If, as Mr. Davis suggests, the US were to expand NAFTA by offering membership to newly democratic Eastern European states, rewarding their advances regarding political freedom (while ignoring the state of their economies), it would be the US which would determine who gets this access. The US will thus indirectly determine who is suitably democratic; cries of neo-imperialism cannot be far off. By utilising non-economic standards, the US, rather than the market, would be picking economic winners and losers at its peril. The FTA approach is not a negotiation but sets a yardstick, giving tremendous tangible reinforcement (in terms of market access) to countries that are doing the right things regarding trade. States with common politico-economic cultures will tend to do better in a free trade grouping than states with unlike backgrounds. This success will, as Mr. Davis says, force the EU core clustered around France and Germany at last to face up to its statist flaws. The FTA approach reinforces positive behaviour while being seen as fair.

It was Mr. Davis who has encouraged me to support a multi-track strategy to the enactment of closer trading relations between the US and the UK. He is entirely correct in that it is at the periphery of the Franco-German core, in Eastern Europe (but also in Ireland, Spain, and the UK) that opportunities exist for the FTA strategy. However, while this multi-tracked approach will allow for successes to influence other countries' decisions about joining (that is, if New Zealand, Australia, Chile and Estonia join there is positive pressure put upon Britain to consider the option), I believe there is something fundamentally wrong with a British policy of constant waiting, to decide down the road if it wishes to join. The tracks should proceed simultaneously. The UK needs to have a significant existential argument about its place in Europe anyway. Mr. Davis's plan is unrealistic as it counts on the US to do too much. In addition, the same argument for waiting can be made just as easily by the Central Europeans or any other country in the world. Those of us who favour the FTA approach do not want to negate British decision-making; it is well past time that the UK decide which path it wishes to take, one as a bridge between Europe and the US, or as a subsumed entity in an emerging European political construct.

Bill Jamieson provides the final piece of the puzzle—the geopolitical underpinnings of the FTA initiative. He is right in that the rude treatment Senator Gramm received in London is illustrative of the height of the mountain that needs climbing for this idea to gain wider acceptance. Here, however, my agreement with Mr. Jamieson ends. Beyond an obvious love of Churchill quotes, I entirely refute Mr. Jamieson's charge of historical romanticism. Having lived and worked in the UK for 7 years, I am aware that the Anglo-American relationship has had its share of ups and downs since the halcyon days of Roosevelt and Churchill. However, to quote Dean Acheson and Suez at me and ignore the Macmillan-Kennedy, Thatcher-Reagan and indeed the Clinton-Blair relationships is to miss the forest for the trees. Indeed, when asked in a November 1999 *Economist* poll who was the UK's most reliable ally in a crisis, 59% of UK respondents said the US, with only 16% giving Europe that compliment. Our arguments (and they are real) are intense, yet family quarrels. They should not obscure the hard, pragmatic realisty that about the third reaction of every American President in a crisis, after 'Good Grief' and 'What is the press reporting?', is to say 'We had better talk to London.' This mutuality of political and economic interests (as well as all the cultural afinities) is so commonplace as often to escape remark. And it is precisely what the US will lose if the UK is subsumed into the EU.

It is not that the UK and the US are not as close as they once were, as Mr. Jamieson suggests; it is just that the US insists on giving the UK such bad geopolitical advice. I totally agree with Mr. Jamieson that the US has consistently pushed Britain further into the EU, supporting the long-held false vision that Britain at the centre of ever-increasing European integration will somehow tame the Franco-German axis by transforming it into a more pro-free trade, pro-free market, pro-American entity. Instead, if anything, the reverse has held true, requiring the mountain climbing of which Mr. Jamieson speaks. Brussels has obliged Britain to support policies that are less pro-free trade, less pro-free market and less pro-American. The Franco-German axis, having converted the Labour Party to the Continental world view as Mr. Jamieson suggests, is poised to make inroads into Britain's different politico-economic culture rather than vice-versa (for example, Britain's adoption of the statist Social Chapter). What America should now say is that the UK will not play a decisive role in what becomes of the EU (as always that will be left to Germany and France) but it can play a critical role in assuring an American-led bloc will maintain its dominance by a wide margin over an integrated statist European rival.

So there is indeed a compelling need to transform the US geopolitical outlook as well, but there are real signs of progress in the United States. From the opinion-forming community (*The Heritage Foundation*, John Bolton, and John O'Sullivan come to mind) to visionaries in the Senate like Senator Gramm, to many members of the Bush team, closer ties with the UK (and alarm about some of the integrationist aspects of the EU) is an idea whose time is coming. It is merely the beginning. As Mr. Jamieson kindly points out, this paper has begun the process of disarming British concern about Britain being isolated if it refuses to accept the euro. The FTA alternative has been put forward. It is now time for Britain to choose an alternative path, for it does not have to be the beginning of the end of the special relationship.

Regulation Without The State...
The Debate Continues

John Blundell
Colin Robinson

The rising tide of government regulation in most countries is provoking a reconsideration of the extent to which the state should lay down rules for others. Self-regulation and other forms of voluntary rule-setting are being examined as substitutes for regulation by government.

Readings 52 begins with a paper by John Blundell and Colin Robinson which analyses the forces behind government regulation, its shortcomings and the scope for voluntary regulation. Seven papers by distinguished commentators on regulation then examine Blundell and Robinson's conclusions.

Contents

The Institute of Economic Affairs
2 Lord North Street, Westminster, London SW1P 3LB
Telephone: 020 7799 3745 Facsimile: 020 7799 2137
E-mail: iea@iea.org.uk Internet: http://www.iea.org.uk   ISBN 0-255 36483-0

£10.00

Transport Policy: The Myth of Integrated Planning

John Hibbs

1. The present government assumes an 'integrated transport policy' is required because integration will not be achieved by market forces. Its policies have an interventionist bias.

2. A fundamental obstacle to introducing a market in transport is the absence of infrastructure pricing for roads.

3. Allocative inefficiency results from Treasury control of road spending. An autonomous funding agency which raised revenue from electronic road use pricing would lead to better decisions. Road and rail infrastructure pricing could come under the same regime.

4. Bus deregulation (outside London) has been successful. In London managers are hampered by bureaucratic controls. Re-regulation of buses should be resisted.

5. Over-hasty privatisation of the railways led to confusion which the present government has made worse. It may be on the road to 'creeping renationalisation'.

6. The functions of the Strategic Rail Authority should be reconsidered; the rail franchising system should be dismantled; and payments for the rail infrastructure should be redesigned to give better investment signals.

7. Subsidies for rural transport have had perverse effects. Any support should be from the level of government closest to the area concerned.

8. Some scope exists for shifting goods movement from road to rail. The key will be to bring the 'provision and pricing of road and rail track under the same regime'.

9. Some government intervention in transport can be justified – for example, supervision of safety standards and investigation of suspected cartels. But, in general, policy should aim to encourage competitive markets in transport.

10. Transport should not be regarded as 'something different' but as an industry best left alone to serve the public.

The Institute of Economic Affairs

2 Lord North Street, Westminster, London SW1P 3LB
Telephone: 0171 799 3745 Facsimile: 0171 799 2137
E-mail: iea@iea.org.uk Internet: http://www.iea.org.uk

£10.00

ISBN 0-255 36493-8

The Modes of Modern Writing

London: Edward
Arnold, 1977

0713162589

Other books by David Lodge

Criticism:

Language of Fiction *(Routledge & Kegan Paul; Columbia University Press)*
The Novelist at the Crossroads *(Routledge & Kegan Paul; Cornell University Press)*
Graham Greene *(Columbia University Press)*
Evelyn Waugh *(Columbia University Press)*
(Editor) Twentieth Century Literary Criticism *(Longman)*
Working with Structuralism *(Routledge & Kegan Paul)*
(Editor) Modern Criticism and Theory *(Longman)*

Novels:

The Picturegoers *(MacGibbon & Kee)*
Ginger, You're Barmy *(MacGibbon & Kee; Doubleday)*
The British Museum is Falling Down *(MacGibbon & Kee; Holt, Rinehart & Winston)*
Out of the Shelter *(Macmillan)*
Changing Places *(Secker & Warburg)*
Small World *(Secker & Warburg)*
Nice Work *(Secker & Warburg)*